The spirit's needs
must drive
the mystery on
while you are
still alive.

feel thee calm pres

First Launch
2016

www.lostinafield.com

Copyright field Basansikis 2016

Contents

It's Go(o)d To Be B(l)ack 1
I Will Kiss You Won Day 2
A Full Score of Honesty 3
There Was Once, There Was Always . 4
If I Only Had Another Minute . . . 5
Again To Thee Angel Song 6
I'm A Person Too 7
Retitle Poem False Jesus 8
Gasoline Obscura 9
Sirens Kept Me From Expression . 10
Ally 11
In Real Life He Lived 12
Not Born Through The Wound . . . 13
Waitless Waiter Awaits Unified . . 14
Make Things Right 15
Naked @ The Writing Desk 16
Ceremony of Your Light 17
The Bukowski Lie 18
Now I Call It Practice 19
The Fourth of Goodbye 20
Remorse Is For Fuckers 21
Off to A Go(o)d Star(t) 22
This Water Is Wine 23
Don't Let It Beat You 24
A Ready Surrender 25
Feel The Compression 26
The Sex Life of Torturers 27
An Act of No Access 28
Inspiration Took A Holiday 29
(I'm) So In Love With Love 30
The Face of Music In Prison . . . 31

Jesus & Santa Claus:
    Gay Love Superstars 32
Cot: A Glimpse of Truth 33
The Sound of A Door Opening 34
Spend The Day In Bed 35
Spirit Flower 36
I Didn't Vote For Your Murder . . . 37
Never Without (Mostly) 38
I Wish For Your Story 39
I'd Trade It Justly 40
Just To Hear Your Voice 41
In Low Light 42
Virtuous Moment 43
Suicide By Potato Chips 44
Complaints Are Restraints 45
Integrity Is Rich 46
Armistice & Resolve 47
Battle or Cattle 48
Save Your End 49
Turning Tables, Unicorn Stables . . 50
Banquet of Recovery 51
If Not This, Have That 52
Eating Fruit Like A Slow Prayer . 53
Nectar In The Air 54
Surface and the Soul 55
Of Course! So Simple 56
How Shall It Begin? (Part 1) 57
Your Source Isn't
a Question (Part 2) 58
Upon Which Fear
To Tread? (Part 3) 59
Creature, Lay Down
Bejeweled (Part 4) 60
Yet To Be Scene 61

Long Ago, Far Away 62
Union Lockout 63
Vertical Lips Sink Ships 64
I'm Such An Asshole 65
How Valuable This Center (of) Time . 66
  Illicit Affair With Mozart's Cousin 67
  And So to Light to Light 68
  Relaxation Is Hard Work 69
  Scratch Those Bug Bites 70
  This Poem Is Invisible 71
  Wish I Gave More 72
  Obscured By Leaves 73
  Witty Title To Placate You 74
  Sympathy Is Pity 75
  Is Isolation Meant As Punishment? . 76
  And They Call This Planet Civilized 77
    Twelve Pages Remain 78
    Stop Seeking Signs 79
    Why Not Bar The Doors? 80
    Come Back & Leave 81
    Out of Control (Try Later) 82
    The Lasting Supper 83
    A Tax On Sales 84
    Know Won Nose for How Long 85
    Too Much Time On Loan 86
      Follow This Truly! 87
      Point of Know Return 88
      Honour Role 89
        Desire 90

Dear Reader,

    I am finally getting this gorgeous little book out to the world. It fell behind the shadow of my impending short story collection, which has hobbled along delayed. The plan has always been to launch the two together. Thankfully, they are now almost ready to fly.

    This book is written in a style known to me as 'Survival Poetry'. It takes the form here of single page free verse prose. These poems are a permission to engage muse, to defend broken dreams and shine.

    When a writer is daunted, it requires great stamina to stay with words and inspiration. The simplicity of Survival Poetry allows a thwarted author to at least drink from some puddles of insight.

    After several years of creative defeat it happened that I went on a trip to Vietnam in February 2015. I engaged the experience while composing this book. It was a step towards artistic rehabilitation & renewal.

    Modest and sincere, quirky and bold, these scrawled poems took form in the welcoming embrace of Vietnam. I am grateful for the gifts I received.

                              x field Basansikis
                     September 2016, Edmonton

wound

It's Go(o)d To Be B(l)ack

The slaves
had all become kings.
The torrent
of their story
ended in the
toilet bowl
of cherries
that life
had inarguably
become.

Tyrants were
bagboys at
the grocery store.
They all had
black eyes
and guilty gazes.

I returned
to myself
with a bouquet
of courageous thought
and a fresh
berry pie
I bought from
the immigrant baker.

"We are all strangers,"
she said smiling,
"until we ignore
God correctly."

I Will Kiss You Won Day

I'm learning you
through the spyglass
of my hope to
connect with you.

Desire, want,
curiosity, awe, lust.
Also, a cardboard box
that has decades
of knowledge
from the behind the scenes
at every slaughterhouse
in the world.

Time ate crayons
and projectile
vomited stale keys.
They opened doors
that only
descended deeper
into the penitentiary.

I waited & waited
& waited & weighted.
No one came to save me.

You can't buy
a lot with crumbs.
The ghosts of
Christmas dinner
wearing thin
paper crowns of
submissive colours.

A Full Score of Honesty

So I returned
and held
medicine in my
mouth that
tasted like
candy.

Every bullet
that needed
to be blocked
was so
heavily taxed
only children
held the capacity
to murder monarchs.

We drowned in
our own cocoons.

Don't hurry
to make excuses!

Be born
into how
you are,
domestic
and holding
Baby Jesus
who needs his
diaper changed.

There Was Once, There Was Always

You were light,
you were
shores of light.

Was it a test
to be offered
brightness
and choose
it as a
reflection?

Pausing
to drink
shadows
that weigh
you down.

Don't drop
your anchor
on the
surface of
the moon.

The illusion
depends on
equal parts
to sever you
from meaning
and to kill Time
to harvest
its flesh.

If I Only Had Another Minute

Remember the story,
the beginning seeking
its reflection in the
quenching water
of your hope.

Wake up forever and
sleep only when your
dreams court
every song,
every corner,
every around
the rainbow.

A return to innocence;
the past clamps
fear onto your
other way round.

A drinking glass
filled with
liquid oxygen.

Finding a needle
in the ashes
of a burnt haystack,
the right way
is signaled
with honour
and the death
of Death's legacy.

Again To Thee Angel Song

You can gain
the same level
of enlightenment
from looking
into a rainy gutter
as you can
from gazing up
a woman's skirt.

Everything is
aflame with
meaning and medicine.

Starved for
an ultimate armistice
you trudge through
the stone walls
of your war
of secrets defeated.

I am rare
to your country
and come with
baskets of flowers
encoded with fragrance.

"The Earth! The Earth!"
They plead in
mirrors, repeating.

I'm A Person Too

Already catching
the angelic splendour
of all my yesterdays
made love to
by honest storms
and keys
on kite strings.

Meaning
in a realm
where most of
the currency
is harvested
from crops
of red rust.

My eyes
drink in the
instructions
on the
"Days-Remaining-
In-Drought"
sign.

Obliterate stink
on the inside;
don't rot and die
decades premature.

People are idiots,
butt I love them.

Retitle Poem False Jesus

Buried in bliss,
don't loan
your future
to the past.

There are better ways
to repay the coins
of accountability
that slipped
from your grasp.

How you were
kept in chains
for a pittance
and a grievous deal
with demons.

It was kind
of you to come
to my wedding.

No one else
was there,
not even
a witness of
spring rain.

My bride,
faceless until,
in the mirror,
my own gaze
reveals you.

Gasoline Obscura

So mistaken
as to sign away
an entire lifetime
of rich potential
and privilege for
the wet sock jubilee.

Really
it is true,
Life is what
you make it.

How silly
to go forward
with the defense
of blindness
by tightly
shutting eyes.

The real thing
to comprehend
is the Band-Aid
apartheid that
keeps a person
a slave to
their own mind.

The past
is a ridiculous
concept to flowers
who only live
to bloom presently.

Sirens Kept Me From Expression

The poem found
on my corpse was
astute and telling,
but not my finest work.

I did appreciate
its metaphors
and hard work wordplay.

However, the best lines
were obscured
by bloodstains.

It's not like
anyone was left
to read it.

The world is
one big riot,
one big massacre,
won big karmic
inevitability.

Hours before
on make-out-point,
my lover and I used
a body to wedge the
wheel of our car,
watching the burning
city in meditation,
like a campfire.

Ally

There is enough time
There is enough
There is
There.

You can't be broken
unless you
want to continue
with the ludicrous
indignity of
giving your
power away.

I'm sitting still
to find myself.

Maybe I will walk
or trot.

Work my way up to
run come save me.

I am
on a
different
continent.

My only
burdens
are that
of belief.

In Real Life He Lived

Tired.
12 hour flight,
no sleep, delays,
but straight ahead mostly.

I'm in Taiwan.
My next flight
leaves in 2 hours.
I wonder if I need
a gourmet coffee.

Survived
the ride over.
Nearing 30 hours awake.
Need a shower.
See old friend
for first time
in 8 years
in around 7 hours.

There is poetry
often to love,
many times
to life,
frequently to hope,
but not always
to a poet
making a
shopping list
of his existence.

Not Born Through the Wound

They turn in
a purpose
that is sometimes
visible and
at other points
hidden from you.

It is clear
in the tension
to medicate
with acceptance.

There are
delightful gifts
to open still.

Stop forcing
the Universe
into an
oblong slot.

Thankful
to be here.
A reunion is soon.
Hungering for
the shore
of enough solace
which can form
a stretcher
to carry God
from war
to obscurity.

Waitless Waiter Awaits Unified

There is
no drought
to recycle
my elegance
to dry wit
riverbed
snowstorms.

Who are
you poem?
What do
you want me
to reveal
of you?

As a poem,
you work the
black shadows
of space.
No stars
befriend you.

Now we are allies,
I have to warn you
of your ending.

"Oh, I don't end,"
you say warmly.
"I was only
borrowed here."

Make Things Right

There are dogs
in the wastepaper
basket.

It's a bore
to be
of anything less
than eternity.

Once you felt
if you didn't write
that you would die.

Now it seems
if you don't die
you won't right
yourself fully.

These stanzas hold
their frigid hands
up to the
prison cell bars
that stretch out
horizontally like
run on sentences.

Drink your
true essence
against the tide
that seeks to
extinguish
your dreams
completely.

Naked @ The Writing Desk

It took
a long fucking time
to make Time less of
a bully cock sucker.

How jealous Time
was of your
intrepid resolves.
He stole them as
signaling stars
and covered
your sky
with bruises.

Writing is a practice
like archery,
like bunkers
to seek amnesty in,
like Archie Bunkers
who's ultimate lesson
was to live alone.

I mourned you
at the pass,
my dead wait soul.

You are raped
while I dwell
inside a fortress.
My castle gates
stained in your
innocence.

Ceremony of Your Light

I did all
my streaking
at a nudist colony.

"field," said the
cock dangler's wife,
"you truly are
a genius, but
nobody will ever
know it until
you assassinate
the hairy apocalypse."

We had so much
to protect us,
the naked truth
and I.

An actual eternity
of infinities
spread out everywhere,
including an
abundant realm of
spectacular significance
found within.

We had a chance,
it's true,
but you can't
bribe the torturer
with empathy's bane.

The Bukowski Lie

Not many messiahs
have it easy
until much later
in their career.

This water I sip
with such pleasure
is sweeter than
scotch or whiskey.

In it I find
just as deep
an intoxication.

How many poets
and humans who
thought themselves
sufficiently capable
of not wasting
your time
have followed
the Bukowski lie?

It's good to
douse your
inner flame
with alcoholism.

How else
can you stand
your own
thin hopes?

Now I Call It Practice

At this point
if you were
to ask me,
I would say
I am as good
as Bukowski.

Maybe we flog sheep
a little differently
and fuck shadows
the same,
but ultimately
I can equal
the Lord
you call upon
for reason.

I wish you knew
the sacrifice
a writer has
to go through to
stay with their art.

I have been
keelhauled
the last 7 years
on the bottom
of a truck
that moved cattle
at night to
slaughterhouses,
thrice removed from
your breakfast table.

The Fourth of Goodbye

We were called
to this moment.

Only here through
the inheritance
of our own
authentic allowance
can we hope that
the bandit "Permission"
will outwit
the authorities.

I sent postcards and
wrote novels best
when there was time
to remember myself.

I was like a
half drunk surgeon
at work on his
own perspectives.

There ARE ugly
elements to Humanity
that manipulate
your attention
and swarm you
with the locust of
Ignorance Incorporated.

Many people died
at the hands of
your greatest hero.

Remorse Is For Fuckers

There is a
slight chill
in the air.

I sit naked
after a day
on the streets
of Hanoi.
I sip water
like port
and listen to
"The Shins".

Quite excellent.

Less than
an hour ago
my travel mate
and I went
to get a
therapeutic massage
for cheap.
I needed the
bathroom first.

I shat like
a democracy upon
the Third World
and had to manually
wipe the inside
of the bowl,
then dramatically left
them all to die.

Off to A Go(o)d Star(t)

The inner channels
of seduction;
how do I
get reception
this far
out to sea?

Weight!
What's this
upon the anchor?
Is it only
a trick of the I?

Here to witness
the last twinkle
reflection of a
star that died
9 million years ago,
but whose light
traveled on.

Once I faced
that I couldn't
quit writing,
that the Devil
truly was best
at cruelty,
I pledged to live
as a killer of pens
with their
black ink blood
my genocide.

This Water Is Wine

Gratitude
is the most
nectarous angel
to breastfeed from.
Although, you
will find her
as a slave
and nurse-mother
to the Master's
wife's token child.

You are weeping.
When I wear
my magic glasses
I can see your
true state.
Your tears are blood
and at nighttime the
halo over your head
illuminates half of
the room you are
chained in.

"I'm not only a fool."
you sputter. "I was
once a Prince
like you."

The rats eat
your crusts of bread
and you are
too tired by life
to flea them.

Don't Let It Beat You

What more
could you ask for,
beside the opportunity
to kiss divinity
all over?

I found direction.
There was an
icing of purpose
on the cake.

That's how we
made our way
out of the catacombs,
singing "Happy Birthday"
and never blowing
the candles out.

Heralded as a genius,
the maggot
in the manger
built structures
of spiritual
architecture
around its ability
to decipher language.

I was never
too keen on
the hidden manifesto
of snails and foreplay.

A Ready Surrender

I wish I could
go back
and affirm
that human with
the soft
breathing token
of my money.

Laughter is
an excellent
antidote for
starving domains,
with some symbolic
and others real.

This was a poem
because it felt
its way across
braille shorelines
and found
where immense,
fool worn meaning
was damned.

"We can always
tell the indignity
from the intrepid,"
said the helmsman.
"There are endless
opportunities in this
dead ocean to drown."

Feel The Compression

There is a vision
of no words,
empty buildings
half built
and sterilized
by lack of
finances.

I laughed
as I recited
the eulogy.
There wasn't
any truth
about the
reincarnation
of unique dues.
These lies
had square wheels
on ice-roads
to prison camps.

Flame that
burns as ointment.

I meditate upon
the unlikely hero.

It was raining
in Hell
and I knew not
to pay faithless
my role
at the gates.

The Sex Life of Torturers

Next to
the ocean
everything
is wet.

The dying
wish to come here,
as sources
of themselves
left clues stashed
when no one
was watching.

Nobody knows
how starving
for intimacy
I am
and none of
the malnourished
grasp how to
play card games
like "go fish".

Many people
have a lot
(of sex).

For them
it isn't even
an issue,
generations in
a tissue.

An Act of No Access

One grows
tired of shadows.
A bright expression
upon the face
of the moon
has me dreaming
of sailing
the cosmos.

Late night silence
fractured by
broken bones
set to music.

Rarity of sustenance,
I long for you
even more
than Nature
of the beast.

Happiness is
a tricky fire
to keep burning.
Is it best
to pop blisters?

I have no noise
to sacrilege my
own memorial by.

No one knows
I'm making progress
a symptom.

Inspiration Took A Holiday

One stage ends
and another opens.
We are citizens
to impermanence.
How vital
it is to
embark often.

Willing hero
decides to
live his own life.

Small fragile
endeavors turn
like keys in
the rusty slots
of stubbornness.

The pretty
young women
on the tour
were blown away
by my poetry
and suggested I write
one about them.

They have enough
people to remind them
how unattainable
a Van Gogh nude is.

(I'm) So In Love With Love

A gentleman
grew a song
like a
rope ladder
of hair
over a condemned
to breath lifetime.

We can't control
these words,
you have to
dance with them.

The stakes are
high for
fighter pilots,
but they are
obtuse cowards
shooting missiles
at civilians
and giving
propaganda handjobs.

The poet is the
real risk taker.
They carry
their words
like dead rabbits
and gamble
entire lives
against God's
indifference.

The Face of Music In Prison

Sometimes a guy
just wants to
suck his thumb.

If the money
is illusory,
then is the debt
also a fabrication?

It is a struggle to
come back to life.

If only the
fish farm captives
knew the precise
place to jump
to reveal themselves
into a cageless ocean.

The meal I starve
for has no calories,
yet makes blood
pulse rocket fuel.

Ahhh, my gracious
banquet of intimacy,
let me savor
your famine ending
glory in courses
to study avid
and relentless.

Jesus & Santa:
Gay Love Superstars

Take your time
and prep the ground.

I am working
your street
like a prostitute.
Leave a candle
to signal
where to spit
the semen.
We'll populate Mars
with dutiful children,
the sons & daughters
of Johns.

If that jungle
never heard
of cement,
this would be
a completely
different tale.

A lot of people
who are successful
are just really
good at thievery.
They use your toaster
to start the fire
that burns
brightly atop
repetition's tower.

Cot: A Glimpse of Truth

I have seen
the coming
of the Lord.

He's woken up
hung over
and is doing
the walk of shame
back home via
two transit busses.

Someone has
felt markered
his forehead
and it reads:

"don't bother"

It's going to
be cold in
the mountains.
Everything is relative.
My yearning for love
is an orphan though;
it has no relatives.

I guess I had
best get to
enjoying being the
solo genius type
written manifesto.

The Sound of A Door Opening

There is a
temptation and gravity
to go toward the
crotch and flatulent
ass of poetry.
I have to be vigilant
to redeem myself
onward to the
higher stairs.
One can't get
too lost in
the smell of odour.
Poets especially.

Yet the key
essential levitation
is toward the flow.
I just see the
mistakes of
'poems that die upon
your bleeding crotch'
and believe a
faster subservience
to fastidiousness
is needed.

If I don't
make the change
there might not
be a parade
to march with
into war.

Spend The Day In Bed

Don't eat the fruit
from the tree.
On the other branch
is a noose.

No sunshine yet
and Day 6
of the trip.
Tonight we have
the semi-hellish
overnight bus
back to the city.
An early morning
flight awaits.

I feel like doing
very little today.
It is quite
misty and cold.
Yesterday we climbed
a mountain graveyard.

A muffled echo
speaks through
damp confines.

The spirit's needs
must drive
the mystery on
while you are
still alive.

Spirit Flower

Torn from
the secret
of my heart
you are
pressed into
my memory
like a living gem.

Behind the
black sky curtain
of night
your effortless grace
pulses like a
star newly born.

In the landscape
of my thoughts
you are a valley
in bloom.

I walk
your pathways
in awe.

I missed
the bright magic
of your
quiet beauty
the moment I left
to travel beyond
the gift
of your
presence.

I Didn't Vote For Your Murder

Lay my story
down in the aisle,
between "nearly dead"
and "you won't
take me alive."

When you travel
internationally,
you are never
exceptionally far
from the interpreter
of your bowels.

Sure, you go in
for a tea or beer,
but it is really
about the royalty
of a functional throne.

I just met
a toilet who was
a people's hero.

Take away
all these
grotesque
expressions
of leadership.

I'm sick to shit
with the rainshower
of the elite.

Never Without (Mostly)

We are always
seeking energy.
To sink to
the ocean floor
is to disavow
a special recognition
required of you.

Form
takes form,
then formless,
formerly your friend.

The ink of
this pen is
an extension
of my connection
to the life force
of the invisible IS.

As I become my own
beacon laureate,
each word is
a step toward
a clearer and clearer
union between us.

I am a channel
for those
who flow with
a resourceful capacity
to liberate themselves
from undertows.

I Wish for Your Story

The reward
was what you
already had,
your heart
that stood
the test and
laid down
no apologies
or excuses
at the altar.

I am missing
a woman I had
a dynamic
exchange with.
Drinkable sunlight
and edible breath like
a platter of fruit.

I am now a thousand
kilometers away
from her and it is
impossible to backtrack
and ache-filled
to yearn.

Still, the gift
is of so sweet
a fragrance
it aligns
wild tigers
to allegiances.

I'd Trade It Justly

You owe it
to yourself to try.

My Time Machine
has expired plates.
I am always
apprehensive about
getting pulled over.

I have
dated Destiny
by the layers
of calcium upon
her landlocked
tombstones.

It is possible
I am close to
a great discovery,
but what if
I don't make it?
What if
I can't find
the endless key
in the finite puzzle?

We are warriors,
you and I.

These injuries were
a universal map
in scars and bruises.

Just to Hear Your Voice

The pain has left...
me humbled.

I can hear
God speaking.
She has a grease
stain on her
American passport;
too much veal
at supper.

Easy to
point fingers;
not so accessible
to truly embrace
every suffering
within memory.

The solution
is to open,
to be available
to oneself and
remain observant
of the world.

If it all
ends tonight,
can you say
your own name
has been
God's name too?

In Low Light

Night after night,
month after month,
the inarguable
humiliation of
going to bed alone.

"You're not wanted"
can be expressed
in the way
others blind
themselves to your
neon open sign.

I can't pay
for electricity
anymore.

The only money
I have left
is two pennies,
one for each I.

No glory,
no stance that
suffers undaunted
like the long drone
of an underground
symphony.

Just wrists
with rivers
beneath them.

Virtuous Moment

Overcast day
and a 50km
scooter mission
one way to
temple ruins.

On the way back,
on a gritty
Vietnam road,
I saw a
blind cripple
walking with
an alms cup
and a stereo speaker
playing traditional
music.

I stopped our caravan
and ran across to
drop a few bills in.

When I turned to come
back over the road,
three locals had
seen what I'd done
and gave me proud
approving smiles
and thumbs up.

My unexpected reward,
better king
than ransom.

Suicide By Potato Chips

So funny,
these defeats.
A bad joke,
an angular cage.

How wonderful
that those
who give
often lament
that they did not
give enough.

And those who are
strictly on the take
fail in their humanity
and grieve inwardly
wanting more still.

My poetry has been
a bit frozen
the last two days.
Medicating depression
with junk food.

There's a
wholesale
on at the
slaughterhouse;
the elephant
that was
in the room.

Complaints Are Restraints

Jesus was a performance artist.

The day he was crucified the mosquitos were very heavy that time of year.

"If I couldn't scratch or shoo them away, what a statement of sacrifice that would be!"

At the final stages, before the unturnable, he got slightly cold feet and employed a brand of insect repellent known as "FARTHUR".

"FARTHUR! Why have you forsaken me!?"

An artist's life force is defeated at 1/1000 of an ounce, one stinging injury at a time.

Integrity Is Rich

I will mark
the honourable
heart with
a speaking altar.

We are flawed,
we are imperfect,
we are what we are.

Deep inside dwells
a tormented energy
that receives, by
the hands of ghosts,
phantom whip strokes
from an unresolved past,
as if the real lashes
were minutes before.

Happiness returns
as a sonnet recited
in a language
you don't understand.

Inside you resolve
in simple equations
to be of
Love's intent
with enough bravery
to make loyal
your personal dawn.

Armistice & Resolve

How shall I
meet you, poetry?
Meek and polluted,
cutting Xs
over snakebites
and spitting venom
in the direction
of my next step?

I have a
combustible desire
that falls just
under the sanctions
of allowable
enticement.

What flower seeks
to blossom
underground?

The Ego pisses
on my flint-stone.
I am a
daylight eclipse.
I was reincarnated
to this life.

The same star
I wish upon
in longing was
my previous form;
delayed light delayed.

Battle or Cattle

There are two things
I am required
to tell you.

One, I think it is
absolutely ridiculous
and tragic that
it is clearly possible
Jesus is a figment
of fabricated control.
It is likely
He never existed.

Secondly,
when I stated
that I am as good
as Bukowski
this is and
is not (yet) true.

The difference is
not necessarily
one of talent or insight.

Rather, he was not
tricked into non-writing.
A lifetime at the
rudder in a tempest
was his statement.

It has yet to be seen
if I will lock myself
in similar dignity.

Save Your End

A water bottle
opened in my satchel
and this pristine book
is now travel wiser.

I was stood up
just now for
a second time
on my travels.
Seems impolite
to mock people
in the triage.

Well, my options
are to feel sorry
for myself or make
something happen,
even if it is just
reforming a life raft
into a houseboat.

Having allowed myself
to feel genuinely
enthusiastic
in contrast is the
worst thing though.

No matter what
you do in prison
you always return
to your selling
feature foreclosed.

Turning Tables, Unicorn Stables

Owe me
of little faith,
how I follow
circles in orbit
of my Jupiter
grievance
instead of
dropping a flare
to ignite
the damp
cosmic confines
of this
unlit sun.

The fox
I was tracking
sprinted behind me
through the meadow
and led me
to water.

We meet up
in an hourglass.

One should not
be too quick
to judge the
Universe's skills
as a thief
to hold you up
at the threshold.

Banquet of Recovery

Eyes and mind
accustomed to
the dark.
Emotions dilate;
brightness slowly
wins you to
your ability
to choose.

The Hornet Queen
offers you mobility,
dragged by threads
through the streets
of exotic charm
by a battalion
of angry wasps.

Today is my
daughter's birthday.
"I can't love
you enough."
What a priceless
honour to have her
in the world;
one of my
greatest successes.

Last night
I lost my life.
I write you here
between worlds.

If Not This, Have That

The concentration
of the tea
opens like a spore
into the
milky water
as I pull
up the bag.

I sit in the
vibrant sunlight
on the rooftop
patio of my hotel.
What were you
looking for
in my poetry?
Have I provided it?

Spitting watermelon
seeds like
well-intentioned
insults over
the railing.

What begins you?
What ends you?
Who are you
without that which
you most desire?

I am a braver
Captain by way of
a good English tea.

Eating Fruit Like A Slow Prayer

God had better
let himself
off the hook.
His suffering
does nothing
for the world
except bind
his spirit.
He is so
viciously alone.
Even a wild
wolverine would
make a better pet
than his despair.

The flags of
Vietnam are
in abundance
everywhere.
They are like poems,
or mantras
of allowance.

If you name
a city after me,
make it a capital
known for compassion.

My love for the
world is my most
persecuted secret.

Nectar In the Air

It was all
directly connected.

Years later they looked
at these words and
thought in reverence:
"The same mind that
moved 3 mountains
from another planet
to ours wrote
this collection.
It's like watching
the play
from backstage."

I had loved you.
Your goodness was
as shimmering
as anyone's.
I was honoured
and made hopeful
by your courage
to be the best you
that you could be.

For I ask you,
what currency
is accepted
in the unknown
other than bills
of crisp truth
and coins of
defiant surrender?

Surface and the Soul

The spoiler
within you
wants to keep
you upon
the shell only.

We need
to dive,
to fall,
to dance,
to make our entrance
into the ceremony
of deeper resonance.

Love energy
is that
sacred delight
that alters
our wasteland
into a vast
wilderness
speckled with
altars.

When we
do not realize
how loved we are
a significance
is lost
like a penny
dropped
into the ocean.

Of Course! So Simple

You bought
and sold slaves,
pulling the Earth
out of orbit
by harnessing
the moon.
It was love
you were seeking.

You gave yourself away
in the hope that someone
would help polish the
handful of grimy gems
no one seemed to notice.
It was love you needed.

The downtrodden,
the perfect failures,
those programed
into shame and guilt
by religion
or scar makers.

All with
their compasses
hungry
to be guided,
not realizing
the destination
was within them.

How Shall It Begin? (Part 1)

I met an oracle today;
at times my internal
was frozen in
delusional flares
of panic.

Being schizophrenic
for some can mean
receiving direct
links to what
seems like God.
Is it all
a trick of
an inflamed ego?

I was nervous.
She runs an
ingenious charity
and is a master baker.
It was hard to
retain the messages,
like hands of worship
knocked away
by bodyguards.

"Ability, will,
opportunity"
is her slogan of
benevolent support.

Your Source Isn't a Question (Part 2)

At least
madness has
some originality.
Greed is as
blatant as rape.

We were given
a tour of the
charity business.
It benefits the deaf.

Likely, I was in
a mild psychosis.
Her personable
presence was
just so direct
it left me
defenseless.

"You can have
the brightest mind
in the world,
but if you are lazy
it doesn't matter."

The pages of
these poems
are filled
upside down
like an
alien sunrise.

Upon Which Fear To Tread? (Part 3)

The oracle was
just being kind.
Perhaps it was
her level of service
that unnerved me.
She stretches
mountain to
shoreline
in the berth
of futures
she helps birth.

"You want people
to be motivated
by reward, not fear.
That doesn't work.
Here we get to
have a lot of fun."

I never like
drinking from
a teacup with
the bag still in it.
The incompleteness
and impoliteness
revolts me.

Maybe my essence is
in the final stages
of brewing before
the bag comes out.

Creature, Lay Down Bejeweled (Part 4)

"Will is the most important part."

End of the tour we exchanged casually one-on-one.
Somehow I referenced my life symbolically:

(Me) "I was pulled from the fire."
(Her) "How long ago?"
(Me) "A year and a half."
(Her, in a motherly, caring and knowing tone) "I'm glad you are safe now."

There was a brief pause and then I replied in closing, "Well, the Universe keeps good people around."

A vignette of insanity and yet a vine whose roots strangle out oppression by shattering shackles with pure form accountability.

Yet To Be Scene

My hotel Trahn Van
moved me into
the penthouse suite,
#406, 4th floor
rooftop legit.

Had been in the
crappy #101 a night,
then a week in #404
that was fairly modest
and awesome enough;
a darker corner
dwelling.

But now I am here
with an actual
writing desk
and a window with
the best view
in the complex.

Ride out with style;
five days remain.

This is the
kind of room that
makes a seeker say
upon arrival,
"Man, you gotta
land a woman here."

Long Ago, Far Away

My favorite moment
of our relationship
was when I was on
magic mushrooms.
My parents suspected
and I called you.

"Come save me."

You arrived and
whisked me away
like a warrior princess.
I never told you
I was high.

I think we went to an
upper class sushi joint
with your mother.
The chef sent an elaborate
dish, complimentary.

During our intimate
teenage acquaintance
I accidentally
betrayed you
a hundred times.
Each time was an accident.

Later, I said I had
tripped over the cat
and that is why the
one of a kind artwork
was smashed to ruins.

Union Lockout

Lee did not really
accustom to
the nuances of
North American
culture.

She threw a
come-as-your-
favorite-sausage
party; it was
awkward.

When she went
to get a ticket
for the ballet
she spent an hour
trying to
barter them down.

Most of her English
was learned from
"Friends" episodes
and she never
quite forgave
Brad Pitt.

Her closest friend
was the doorman
and even he
punched the clock
senseless.

Vertical Lips Sink Ships

Today is my
half birthday.
I am forty
point five.

Looking at the
unintentionally
seductive English
woman next table over
is half a gift.

I get the empty box
that the present
might have come in.

I have also
fallen in love
with Vietnam.
She is stunning,
a subtle and
overt beauty.

I wonder if
anyone will
ever care
that my eyes
are green.
Maybe an
off-worlder
upon whose planet
green isn't
a colour.

I'm Such An Asshole

I just saw
a poster
advertisement
of an Asian
body builder.
He looked like
a piece of bacon
with a taut face.

Last year I saw
on the internet
the story of
a waitress
who was given a
thousand dollar tip-
"So you can make
it to Italy."

I bet you
ten-to-one
she never went.

Excuses grow
like erections.
It wasn't money
that stopped her.

It was an
inflammation
of the
mediocrity gland.

How Valuable This Center (of) Time

Spin the wheel
and choose a muse.
Wishing somehow the
earnest sincerity of
my heart could be
recognized and uplifted
in something resembling
intimate love.

Touch the inside
of your body.
Your organs have
never seen sunlight.
Those bones are dormant
landmines in a war whose
consequence is shared.

My uncle owns
the metaphor shop.
I have always been
his favorite nephew.
I select my words
for free as
candy and fruit.

The poet's victory must
be glimpsed over rooftops.

Inequity and sin
may seam cheap,
but certainly
not affordable.

Illicit Affair With Mozart's Cousin

I am in Hoi An,
a bedazzling
tourist town.
The people of
this country are
such a discovery,
like waking to
the aroma of freshly
baked bread
at the foot
of your bed.

By good fortune
I have been
adopted and befriended
by some UK locals
who work and
live here.

I may not have
ignited any romance,
but I have
kindle sparked
dynamite bank heists.

The adventure calls
for brothers as kin
to restore
within themselves
the rightful
heir of Princes.

And So to Light to Light

Fuck. My solitude
just got soiled.
This guy has
the whole restaurant
to sit in and
he goes straight
across from me.

Oh well,
maybe we are friends.

It's a big country,
I can share it.

Down here
on the street
the window of
my hotel room
looks like the
office of a
happiness architect.

(Time elapses)

Human connection
is sustenance.
He invited himself over.
We had a great chat.
Breakfast and two coffees
was 71,000 dong,
yet I leave richer
than when I arrived.

Relaxation Is Hard Work

Naked time
in the hotel room
is a unified thing.
You get to have your
own private state
within the
undiscovered country's
invitation to
be vulnerable.

In a few minutes
I will swim
in the pool.
I am not in a rush.
I cherish this
sensitivity.
A personal meeting
between me and myself;
an aura can breathe.

Music is playing
and I have tea.

Sometimes I think
of the woman
far back home
whom I desire
to know.

At certain points
I give zero fucks
that I never
get to fuck.

Scratch Those Bug Bites

The aliens can get
a million times
more efficiency
from oil than any
Earth bound engine.

They are greedy
to live in space.
To them
we are cockroaches
that can use
language.

In a binding array,
our planet has
been raped like
a young deity virgin.

The final act is to
cut her tongue out.

In their ships
on the dark side
of the moon,
they pass the time
by masturbating into
each other's mouths.

In a perfect world
penetration
is only foreplay.

This Poem Is Invisible

This will
read strangely,
but sometimes
my foot sweat smells
sweetly pungent
like a vagina.

Why point fingers
of blame when you
can sniff them
unintentionally as a
postcard of memory.

"Fingers and toes,
forty things we share."

I am curious.
Churches of hypocrisy
think themselves
the most holy;
too virtuous
to use pull out
birth control
on the Krishna
in the mirror.

Religion is caste dice.

Oh, my beloved
impoverished,
you die by seeing
the world through
snake eyes.

Wish I Gave More

I want to write
the quietest poem
in the world.
More silent
than sunlight,
with the footfall
of mice over marble.

I want you
to forgive me
by the mute song
of this poem
unfolding.

I wish for
its stanzas
to point to
hidden lepers
made outcast
in your journey;
they all have
your own face.

Heal them!
Bring them water!
Why pay taxes
in the currency of
bleeding wound gardens?

The only messiah
you need is you
as your genuine self.

Obscured By Leaves

In the streets that
long for stillness
I am courting witness
like a pilgrim.
The trial has been hard to
endure and at times cruel.
I need someone to
clasp my hand as I
make my own verdict.

You pay at the tollbooth
with attention and iced
coffee comes later as a
preemptive dessert.

There are some people who
claim to be able to see
angels walking among us.

Rumors swell, like
honourable black eyes,
that others can decipher
ghosts in waking hours.

Here in the
land of the living,
enlightenment means
seeing each person
as their parents have,
gazing upon the
most triumphant
source of beauty
in all of Existence.

Witty Title to Placate You

Working with
bad math formulas.
This humble pi
goes on forever.

Ready for
my trip to end.
No female co-star
in this movie.
Just cameo appearances
by women doing
product placement.

Decided in the
last hour to ditch
this town a
day earlier.

Paying the bill
pops a bubble.

Everything ends
and everything
comes with a price.

Good thing you're
so God damned
entertained
by my poetry.

Thank fucking Christ!

Sympathy Is Pity

Here in the
closing dark
of consequences
I am burdened
by the slow wit
of accountability.

Each day
like clockwork
the staff was paid
in poker chips.
You could almost
hear the failure
take charge.

It was effortless
to be deaf to things
like conscience.

Nobody knew
the odds better.
If you worked
to fool yourself
you could lean
your bets up
against them.

Water doesn't
run uphill,
unless it is
humans escaping
80% slaughter.

Is Isolation Meant As Punishment?

Sunny day,
looks nice,
don't care.

After breakfast
I brought a plate
of fresh fruit
and pastries
up to my room,
balanced on
this book like a
wide-eyed idiot.

Top of the stairs
took the bait and went
to steal a water from the
cleaning lady's supplies.

The plate fell off
and shattered.
I used this sacred
text as a broom,
now it's holier.

Minutes before the
lobby girl commented
on my watermelon.

"Yeah, I want to eat it
off of your stomach."
I murmured just audible
as I walked away.

And They Call This Planet Civilized

It is near the
end of my trip.

I took to going out
without my writing.
Sitting with myself
in complete neutrality,
like an abused wife
who's husband just died.

I rented a
motorcycle today.
Truly adventured about.
Witnessed some
genuine Vietnam.

Found the
fisherman's harbour.
Backcountry paths
to the waterside.
Rare and perfect
sunlight.

I saved myself today,
by way of having fun.

I could of gotten lost
and never resurfaced,
a graveyard
under landslides.

Twelve Pages Remain

There is a mantra
you should know:

Nothing can be
denied you,
except what you
deny yourself.

Each plateau
comes with a cost.
Depression is way
too expensive
an addiction.

If you only
knew what is
robbed of you.

The Universe
can see it.
What you could
easily become.
Only the
hardest choices
stand between.

Occupy your life.
Don't be a pawn
to your lower self.

Pardon me! Please.

Stop Seeking Signs

I am in a room
of parking lots.
Nothing is permanent.
My soul works
the pay booth.

Sometimes people
exchange with me
like I am invisible,
as a machine
to be punched.

All the Masters
have stayed here.
They found the door,
"The Exit Inside".

Potential is not
a dirty word.

God was a
prostitute
you did or
did not employ.

These riddles are
like x-rays
over my essence.

See how I've
swallowed the ocean
hook, line and sinker?

Why Not Bar the Doors?

I have stood
in the tide
of the decline,
white people
partying while
the world burns.

I have fostered
bright signals
from behind the
moon's regret.

Sometimes it is best
to untether poetry
and chase wolves
out of habit.

Words, words,
sometimes words.

A drunk celebration
in an alien nation.

They didn't come.
Not ever really.

I had Goddess
trading cards
and the bubblegum
was stale.

Come Back & Leave

The friend of the
world is coming.
The friend of the
world is near.

Everything has
a beginning,
middle and friend.

Your story is only
half worked out
if there is
no friend to
your sorrows.

I see how
lucky I had it
in Hoi An.
I was spoiled.
Here in Danang
the streets are
lockouts and the
hotel staff welcome
you like wet rain.
The wedding is
all bill and
no ceremony.

Seemingly lacking
ninjas, the rooftops
in this city
have no poetic
footfall upon them.

Out of Control (Try Later)

I was shocked
by the size of
my belly in the
mirror just now.

I have become
the unintentional
Mayor figurehead
in the demographic
of fat people.

I didn't even
vote for myself!

Thankfully, my time
in Danang is short.
Even if I hate it,
only 1.5 days remain.

Poems were
led as goats to
the butcher's knife.

The memory of
mountain path freedom
was fresh upon them.

I lay unlaid
upon the tracks,
waiting to get hit
by some train
of thought.

The Lasting Supper

The reader got
a little irritable
with my work:

"Yeah, I get it,
you're:
Horny, Lonely
Hungry, Depressed.
You are moving
toward your spirit.
Aren't we all?"

It was hard
to become happy.
A perfectly fitting
suit made from flags,
white flags
of surrender.

This city got kinder,
defenses down the hatch.
My trip has been a
beauty full offering.
A parade of indifference
is still a parade.

I had a bride called
the Present Moment
and I insisted on tying
the laces of her shoes
lest she stumble
on without me.

A Tax On Sales

In the closing scenes
I adjusted my course
as the wind turned
its back on me.

The soft spoken words
of the waitress asking,
"You finished?"
in my ear just now
were among the
Top 5 most intimate
things I experienced
in Vietnam.

I was going to write
a poem to leave
behind the painting
in my hotel room,
but it felt too
contrived to compose.

My poetry was
all breadcrumbs;
empty busy streets
and birds happy
in their cages.

I want to show you
how grateful I am.
Look here!
In my cupped hands,
Eternity... mostly sort of.

Know Won Nose
For How Long

Leaving Vietnam
on the trail
of my wholeness.
I am at the airport
where it all began
3.3 weeks ago.

They say that it is
all within you,
everything you need.
That it is an error
to seek externally
for the ultimate
bridge to essence.

You are in a
duel with duality.
You have every chance
to either complain
or be grateful.

A fish in a
waterless bucket
stares at you lidless.
The air is filled
with razors that
cut away life force.
Through the jungle
cut me a way,
as I reconcile with
what sentence remains.

Too Much Time On Loan

Here, on the other
side of the world,
I have traveled
far to find myself.

The moon is made
a mirror only by the
brilliance of the sun.
Otherwise you are
staring into
oceans of shadow.

I imagine I shall
endeavor in life
to tear down the walls
of financial tyranny.

But what of the
inequality that
dwells within?

You have to let go
in actions and walk away
by walking toward
your vision.

Hardcore romantic
held in check by
lonely times.
A holodeck paradise
ebbs inverted
as an attrition
veiling bondage.

Follow This Truly!

There is something
uniquely precious
within you,
infinitely rare.

Almost no one knows
of the source of
what you long to do.
It calls to you now
only infrequently
as you have buried
yourself dazedly under
thick blankets, soiled
with energetic disease.

Sometimes you
glimpse it.
For a moment your
heart breathes and
your essence rejoices.

You need courage!
You need clarity!
You need to know
that you are
deeply loved for you
and nothing else.

Please don't fail
yourself and the world.
Give us a passing grade.
Make your mother proud.

Point of Know Return

We left Asia
at midnight on the
Chinese New Year.

Outside my window
awaiting takeoff
I saw a dozen
different fireworks
displays.

So much love to give.
A hunger and
vicious thirst
for feminine light,
denied denied denied.
Yet I won't drown
completely in what
I don't have.

Judge me if you want to.
I am a lover with
no shore except the
consolation prizes of
existence, enlightenment,
purpose, friends, health
and family.

My potential
is limitless.
I court you
openly, Redemption.
We are each
other's teachers.

Honour Role

Punk rock on
my headphones
and the mercifully
short final flight
to Edmonton half done.

Got a special ally on
the other end waiting
to offer a victory ride
back into town.

I hope you found
a few heart tokens
here in this
abysmal bliss and
tortured triumph.

This may be the
only book of mine
you ever read.
Resuscitation can be
a fun and lively art.

I place sleeping cats at
your feet and dust your
mantle with the
feathers of peacocks
who were often shunned
for their raw humility.

In a thousand breaths
you will have forgotten
this poem completely.

Desire

In moments
I will lay
freshly showered
into my clean
sheets bed.

Truly alive is the
thing to strive for.

Elements of identity
gather refrains of
speaking counsel.

My compass has
been upgraded.

Tomorrow I wake
within my
Canadian realm,
but I am new
and wiser to my
own diligence.

Thank you so much
for linking with my
words and feelings here.

I wrote these poems
to love life and in
doing so, love you,
my cherished recipient
of kindred codes
and broken odes.

Made in the USA
Charleston, SC
27 November 2016